# Grammar
# Practice Book

## Grade 1

**SCHOOL PUBLISHERS**

www.harcourtschool.com

# Contents

# Contents

Grammar Practice Book
© Harcourt • Grade 1

Name _____

▶ **Write each sentence correctly.**

**1.** you nap

_____
- - - - - - - - - - - - - - - - - - - - - - - - - - - - - -
_____

_____

**2.** i see my cat

_____
- - - - - - - - - - - - - - - - - - - - - - - - - - - - - -
_____

_____

**3.** she ran to me

_____
- - - - - - - - - - - - - - - - - - - - - - - - - - - - - -
_____

_____

**4.** dad has a van

_____
- - - - - - - - - - - - - - - - - - - - - - - - - - - - - -
_____

**Grammar Practice Book**
© Harcourt • Grade 1 • Book 1

▶ **Circle each group of words that is a sentence.**

1. the jam

2. sam ran

3. tag

4. we tap

5. i sat

▶ **Write the circled sentences correctly.**

6. _____

7. _____

8. _____

▶ **Circle each group of words that is a sentence.**

1. pam sat down

2. the man

3. i look at a cat

4. ran

5. they

▶ **Add words to the others to make sentences. Write the sentences correctly.**

6. _____
_____

7. _____
_____

8. _____
_____

**Grammar Practice Book**
© Harcourt • Grade 1 • Book 1

▶ **Add words to make each word or group of words into a sentence. Write the sentences correctly.**

**1.** ran

_____

- - - - - - - - - - - - - - - - - - - - - - - - - - -

_____

**2.** we

_____

- - - - - - - - - - - - - - - - - - - - - - - - - - -

_____

**3.** the cat

_____

- - - - - - - - - - - - - - - - - - - - - - - - - - -

_____

**4.** i like

_____

- - - - - - - - - - - - - - - - - - - - - - - - - - -

_____

**5.** has

_____

- - - - - - - - - - - - - - - - - - - - - - - - - - -

_____

Name _____

► **Write each group of words in the correct order to make a sentence. Write the sentences correctly.**

**1.** the nap can cat

_____

- - - - - - - - - - - - - - - - - - - - - - - - - - - - - -

_____

_____

**2.** dad a van ran to

_____

- - - - - - - - - - - - - - - - - - - - - - - - - - - - - -

_____

_____

**3.** the bag Sam has

_____

- - - - - - - - - - - - - - - - - - - - - - - - - - - - - -

_____

_____

**4.** Max wag can

_____

- - - - - - - - - - - - - - - - - - - - - - - - - - - - - -

_____

**Grammar Practice Book**
© Harcourt • Grade 1 • Book 1

**Name** _____

▶ **Circle each group of words that is in the correct order.**

1. Pam has a cat.

2. like we tag

3. rat the had jam

4. I am sad.

5. mad I am

▶ **Write the other sentences correctly.**

_____

6. _____

_____

7. _____

_____

8. _____

**Grammar Practice Book**
© Harcourt • Grade 1 • Book 1

▶ **Circle each group of words that is in the correct order. Write each sentence correctly.**

**1.** dad helps me bat

_____

- - - - - - - - - - - - - - - - - - - - - - - - - - - -

_____

_____

**2.** cat there ran the

_____

- - - - - - - - - - - - - - - - - - - - - - - - - - - -

_____

_____

**3.** I had a tan hat

_____

- - - - - - - - - - - - - - - - - - - - - - - - - - - -

_____

_____

**4.** Max a sees map

_____

- - - - - - - - - - - - - - - - - - - - - - - - - - - -

_____

Name _____

▶ **Write each sentence correctly.**

**1.** down cat the sat

_____

- - - - - - - - - - - - - - - - -

_____

**2.** had nap a he

_____

- - - - - - - - - - - - - - - - -

_____

**3.** in rat a ran

_____

- - - - - - - - - - - - - - - - -

_____

▶ **Write a sentence that tells what happens next.**

_____

- - - - - - - - - - - - - - - - -

**4.** _____

_____

- - - - - - - - - - - - - - - - -

_____

**Grammar Practice Book**
© Harcourt • Grade 1 • Book 1

▶ **Write the naming part of each sentence.**

**1.** I sat down.

_____
- - - - - - - - - - - - - - - - - -
_____

**2.** Dad sat down, too.

_____
- - - - - - - - - - - - - - - - - -
_____

**3.** Bill will sit here.

_____
- - - - - - - - - - - - - - - - - -
_____

**4.** My dog sits there.

_____
- - - - - - - - - - - - - - - - - -
_____

**5.** They like my dog.

_____
- - - - - - - - - - - - - - - - - -
_____

**Grammar Practice Book**
© Harcourt • Grade 1 • Book 1

▶ **Circle the naming part of each
sentence. Then write each sentence
correctly.**

**1.** Bill is at camp

_____

- - - - - - - - - - - - - - - - - - - - - - -

_____

**2.** Kim is his pal

_____

- - - - - - - - - - - - - - - - - - - - - - -

_____

**3.** she is at camp

_____

- - - - - - - - - - - - - - - - - - - - - - -

_____

**4.** they see sand

_____

- - - - - - - - - - - - - - - - - - - - - - -

_____

**5.** the two pals dig

_____

- - - - - - - - - - - - - - - - - - - - - - -

_____

▶ **Circle each group of words that is a sentence.**

**1.** The man has a mask.

**2.** has a mitt.

**3.** will bat.

**4.** can hit.

**5.** She ran fast.

▶ **Now add naming parts to the other groups of words to make complete sentences. Write your sentences correctly.**

**6.** _____

_____

**7.** _____

_____

**8.** _____

Name _____

**Naming Parts of Sentences**

**Lesson 3**

▶ **Add a naming part from the box to complete each sentence.**

| Liz | We | I | Dan |

1. _____ will go on a raft.

2. _____ can help lift it.

3. _____ has a map.

4. _____ get on.

▶ **Write a sentence that tells what happens next. Write your sentence correctly. Then circle the naming part.**

5. _____

12

**Grammar Practice Book**
© Harcourt • Grade 1 • Book 1

▶ **Underline the telling part of each sentence. Then write the sentence correctly.**

**1.** Dad bats now

_____

- - - - - - - - - - - - - - - - - - - - - - - -

_____

**2.** he will hit it

_____

- - - - - - - - - - - - - - - - - - - - - - - -

_____

**3.** Jan hit the ball

_____

- - - - - - - - - - - - - - - - - - - - - - - -

_____

**4.** she ran fast

_____

- - - - - - - - - - - - - - - - - - - - - - - -

_____

**5.** Ted sits down

_____

- - - - - - - - - - - - - - - - - - - - - - - -

**Grammar Practice Book**
© Harcourt • Grade 1 • Book 1

▶ **If the group of words is a complete sentence, underline the telling part.**

1. Kim and Bill dig in the sand.

2. they

3. Pat and I

4. We ran past Kim and Bill.

5. I

▶ **Now add telling parts to the other groups of words to make sentences. Write the sentences correctly.**

_____

6. _____

_____

7. _____

_____

8. _____

**Grammar Practice Book**
© Harcourt • Grade 1 • Book 1

Name _____

► **Look at the picture. Draw a line to match the naming parts of sentences with the telling parts.**

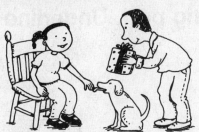

1. I                                    has a gift.

2. Dad                                 licks my hand.

3. Wag                                 sit down.

► **Write the sentences correctly.**

4. _____

_____

5. _____

_____

6. _____

**Grammar Practice Book**
© Harcourt • Grade 1 • Book 1

▶ **Write two sentences about the
characters in the picture. Make sure
each sentence is written correctly, with a
naming part and a telling part. Underline
the telling part.**

1. _____

2. _____

16

▶ **Write these telling sentences correctly.**

**1.** a cat is in the box

_____

- - - - - - - - - - - - - - - - - - - - - - - - -

_____

**2.** a dog is on the mat

_____

- - - - - - - - - - - - - - - - - - - - - - - - -

_____

**3.** the cat sits

_____

- - - - - - - - - - - - - - - - - - - - - - - - -

_____

**4.** the dog naps

_____

- - - - - - - - - - - - - - - - - - - - - - - - -

_____

▶ **Circle each telling sentence that is written correctly.**

1. The ants lift the rock.

2. the pigs dig

3. The cat has milk.

4. he is hot.

5. A pot is on the rack

▶ **Write the other sentences correctly.**

6. _____

7. _____

8. _____

**Grammar Practice Book**
© Harcourt • Grade 1 • Book 1

▶ **Add words to make a telling sentence.**
**Then write the sentence correctly.**

**1.** the dog

_____

- - - - - - - - - - - - - - - - - - - - - - - - - - -

_____

_____

**2.** in a box

_____

- - - - - - - - - - - - - - - - - - - - - - - - - - -

_____

_____

**3.** ran fast

_____

- - - - - - - - - - - - - - - - - - - - - - - - - - -

_____

_____

**4.** She has

_____

- - - - - - - - - - - - - - - - - - - - - - - - - - -

_____

▶ **Write these telling sentences correctly.**

   **1.** dogs can dig

   _____

   - - - - - - - - - - - - - - - - - - - - - - - - - -

   _____

   _____

   **2.** cats are soft

   _____

   - - - - - - - - - - - - - - - - - - - - - - - - - -

   _____

   _____

   **3.** a fox is fast

   _____

   - - - - - - - - - - - - - - - - - - - - - - - - - -

   _____

   _____

   **4.** an ant is not big

   _____

   - - - - - - - - - - - - - - - - - - - - - - - - - -

   _____

▶ **Write a telling sentence of your own.**

   _____

   - - - - - - - - - - - - - - - - - - - - - - - - - -

   **5.** _____

Name _____

▶ **Write each question correctly.**

**1.** how are you

_____

- - - - - - - - - - - - - - - - - - - - - - -

_____

**2.** where is Jim

_____

- - - - - - - - - - - - - - - - - - - - - - -

_____

**3.** what can we do

_____

- - - - - - - - - - - - - - - - - - - - - - -

_____

**4.** will you come

_____

- - - - - - - - - - - - - - - - - - - - - - -

_____

21

▶ **Circle each question that is written correctly.**

    1. Can you pack the bag?

    2. where is Ann?

    3. will we go soon?

    4. Will you pack a mitt?

    5. where is the map.

    6. is this the map.

▶ **Now write the other questions correctly.**

7. _____

_____

8. _____

_____

9. _____

_____

10. _____

Grammar Practice Book
© Harcourt • Grade 1 • Book 1

▶ **Read each pair of sentences. Circle the sentence that is a question. Then write the question correctly.**

1. where are you          I am at home

   _____

   - - - - - - - - - - - - - - - - - - - - - - - - - - -

   _____

   _____

2. Rick has a ball          will he kick it

   _____

   - - - - - - - - - - - - - - - - - - - - - - - - - - -

   _____

   _____

3. Todd ran to the ramp          where is the ramp

   _____

   - - - - - - - - - - - - - - - - - - - - - - - - - - -

   _____

   _____

4. can I have a mop          I like to help

   _____

   - - - - - - - - - - - - - - - - - - - - - - - - - - -

   _____

**Grammar Practice Book**
© Harcourt • Grade 1 • Book 1

Name _____

▶ **Write each question correctly.**

1. how can he help

   _____

   - - - - - - - - - - - - - - - - - - - - - - -

   _____

2. what can she fix

   _____

   - - - - - - - - - - - - - - - - - - - - - - -

   _____

3. will he fix it

   _____

   - - - - - - - - - - - - - - - - - - - - - - -

   _____

4. who is she

   _____

   - - - - - - - - - - - - - - - - - - - - - - -

   _____

▶ **Write a question about the picture.**

5. _____

   - - - - - - - - - - - - - - - - - - - - - - -

   _____

**Grammar Practice Book**
© Harcourt • Grade 1 • Book 1

▶ **Write these exclamations correctly.**

**1.** help me

_____
- - - - - - - - - - - - - - - - - - - - - - - - - - - - -
_____
_____

**2.** my dog is lost

_____
- - - - - - - - - - - - - - - - - - - - - - - - - - - - -
_____
_____

**3.** oh no

_____
- - - - - - - - - - - - - - - - - - - - - - - - - - - - -
_____
_____

**4.** come home

_____
- - - - - - - - - - - - - - - - - - - - - - - - - - - - -
_____
_____

**5.** thank you

_____
- - - - - - - - - - - - - - - - - - - - - - - - - - - - -
_____
_____

▶ **Circle each sentence that is an exclamation.**

1. He will help.

2. Help!

3. Go to bed!

4. I will go to bed.

5. Let's go!

▶ **Think of other exclamations. Write them correctly.**

6. _____

7. _____

8. _____

**Grammar Practice Book**
© Harcourt • Grade 1 • Book 2

► **Write the first word of each sentence the correct way. Put a period (.), question mark (?), or exclamation point (!) at the end.**

get    Get

_____

- - - - - - - - - - - - - - - - - - -

1. _____ up _____

_____

do    Do

_____

- - - - - - - - - - - - - - - - - - -

2. _____ you like milk _____

_____

max    Max

_____

- - - - - - - - - - - - - - - - - - -

3. _____ will go home _____

_____

Let    let

_____

- - - - - - - - - - - - - - - - - - -

4. _____ go _____

▶ **Look at the picture. Write exclamations to go with the picture.**

1. _____

_____

2. _____

_____

3. _____

_____

4. _____

▶ **Write a noun to complete each
sentence.**

_____
- - - - - - - - - - - - - - - - -

**I.** Mom went to the _____.

_____

_____
- - - - - - - - - - - - - -

**2.** Dad is at the _____.

_____

_____
- - - - - - - - - - - - - - -

**3.** I like Ross and _____.

_____

_____
- - - - - - - - - - - - - - - -

**4.** We went camping at the _____.

_____

_____
- - - - - - - - - - - - - -

**5.** Tess and _____ are here now.

29

▶ **Look at each picture. Write a noun that names each person or place.**

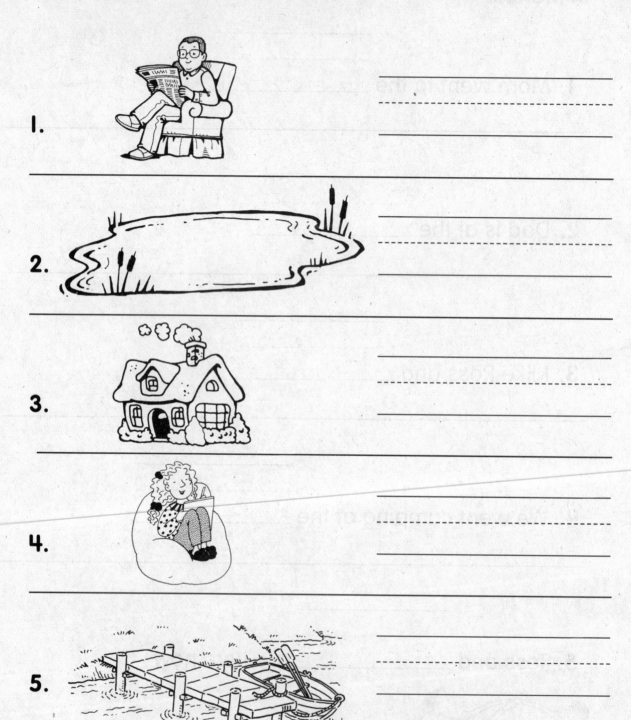

1.

_____
- - - - - - - - - - - - - - - - - -
_____

2.

_____
- - - - - - - - - - - - - - - - - -
_____

3.

_____
- - - - - - - - - - - - - - - - - -
_____

4.

_____
- - - - - - - - - - - - - - - - - -
_____

5.

_____
- - - - - - - - - - - - - - - - - -
_____

▶ **Write a noun to complete each sentence.**

_____

1. I see _____ at the pen.

_____

2. Rick and _____ go to the mall.

_____

3. Rob is at _____ .

_____

4. Jan and _____ are in the tent.

_____

5. I ran to the _____ .

Name _____

▶ **Look at the picture. Write two sentences to go with the picture. Use nouns that name places and people.**

1. _____
   ----------------------------------------
   _____
   ----------------------------------------
   _____

2. _____
   ----------------------------------------
   _____
   ----------------------------------------
   _____

**Grammar Practice Book**
© Harcourt • Grade 1 • Book 2

▶ **Read each sentence. Write the noun that names an animal or a thing.**

_____
- - - - - - - - - - - - - - - - -

1. We run past the tent. _____

_____

- - - - - - - - - - - - - - - - -

2. We rest on a log. _____

_____

_____
- - - - - - - - - - - - - - - - -

3. I see an ant. _____

_____

_____
- - - - - - - - - - - - - - - - -

4. Jack picks up a bug. _____

_____

_____
- - - - - - - - - - - - - - - - -

5. The dog sniffs it. _____

▶ **Underline the nouns in the box that name animals. Circle the nouns that name things.**

| | | | | |
|---|---|---|---|---|
| bed | bus | dog | duck | gift |
| mask | moth | pig | plant | rat |

▶ **Use a noun from the box to complete each sentence.**

1. I want to get a _____.

_____

2. I don't want a _____.

_____

3. I slept on a _____.

_____

4. I will not step on a _____.

**Grammar Practice Book**
© Harcourt • Grade 1 • Book 2

▶ **Circle all the nouns in the box.**

| | | | | |
|---|---|---|---|---|
| ball | big | cat | flag | got |
| hog | nest | pup | rat | sit |

▶ **Choose a noun from the box to complete each sentence. Write the sentences correctly.**

1. A _____ sat on a log.

   _____

   - - - - - - - - - - - - - - - - - - - - - - - - - - - - -

   _____

2. That is my _____.

   _____

   - - - - - - - - - - - - - - - - - - - - - - - - - - - - -

   _____

3. The dog has a _____.

   _____

   - - - - - - - - - - - - - - - - - - - - - - - - - - - - -

   _____

4. The _____ ran fast.

   _____

   - - - - - - - - - - - - - - - - - - - - - - - - - - - - -

   _____

**Grammar Practice Book**
© Harcourt • Grade 1 • Book 2

Name _____

▶ **Circle the nouns. Then write four sentences. Use a noun from the box in each sentence.**

| | | |
|---|---|---|
| dig | dog | fox |
| hand | has | map |
| raft | sled | soft |

1. _____

2. _____

3. _____

4. _____

▶ **Write each group of words correctly.**

**1.** two ball

_____
- - - - - - - - - - - - - - - - - - - - - - - -
_____

_____

**2.** one hands

_____
- - - - - - - - - - - - - - - - - - - - - - - -
_____

**3.** one masks

_____
- - - - - - - - - - - - - - - - - - - - - - - -
_____

**4.** two egg

_____
- - - - - - - - - - - - - - - - - - - - - - - -
_____

_____

**5.** one bumps

_____
- - - - - - - - - - - - - - - - - - - - - - - -
_____

**6.** two sled

_____
- - - - - - - - - - - - - - - - - - - - - - - -
_____

_____

**7.** one moths

_____
- - - - - - - - - - - - - - - - - - - - - - - -
_____

**8.** one plants

_____
- - - - - - - - - - - - - - - - - - - - - - - -
_____

Name _____

▶ **Write the word that names each picture.**

1.

_____
- - - - - - - - - - - - - -
_____

2.

_____
- - - - - - - - - - - - - -
_____

3.

_____
- - - - - - - - - - - - - -
_____

4.

_____
- - - - - - - - - - - - - -
_____

▶ **Choose a picture and write a sentence about it.**

_____
- - - - - - - - - - - - - - - - - - - - - - - - - -

5. _____

_____
- - - - - - - - - - - - - - - - - - - - - - - - - -
_____

**Grammar Practice Book**
© Harcourt • Grade 1 • Book 2

▶ **Write each sentence correctly.**

**1.** I have six stamp.

_____

- - - - - - - - - - - - - - - - - - - - - - -

_____

_____

**2.** Russ has a pens

_____

- - - - - - - - - - - - - - - - - - - - - - -

_____

_____

**3.** I have one bags

_____

- - - - - - - - - - - - - - - - - - - - - - -

_____

_____

▶ **Write a sentence that tells about more than one thing.**

_____

- - - - - - - - - - - - - - - - - - - - - - -

**4.** _____

_____

- - - - - - - - - - - - - - - - - - - - - - -

_____

▶ **Look around the room. What do you see? Write sentences that tell how many you see of some things.**

_____

1. _____

_____

_____

2. _____

_____

_____

3. _____

_____

_____

**Grammar Practice Book**
© Harcourt • Grade 1 • Book 2

▶ **Read the sentences. Circle the titles and special names. Write the sentences correctly.**

**1.** mark swung a bat

_____
- - - - - - - - - - - - - - - - - - - - -
_____

**2.** jan gets a cat

_____
- - - - - - - - - - - - - - - - - - - - -
_____

**3.** miss smith is tall

_____
- - - - - - - - - - - - - - - - - - - - -
_____

**4.** mr webb packed

_____
- - - - - - - - - - - - - - - - - - - - -
_____

▶ **Circle each sentence that is written correctly.**

**1.** mr. Wall sang a song.

**2.** We all liked the song.

**3.** miss fox helped us.

**4.** We sang at school.

**5.** We sang with mr. rand.

▶ **Write the other sentences correctly.**

**6.** _____

_____

_____

**7.** _____

_____

**8.** _____

_____

▶ **Circle the special names and titles.**

> he   rick   man   mr ling   dr bond   she   beth

▶ **Look at the pictures. Complete each sentence using a special name from the box. Write each special name correctly.**

_____

1. _____ likes to fish.

_____

2. _____ helps pets get well.

3. We met _____

_____

4. _____ sings for our class.

**Grammar Practice Book**
© Harcourt • Grade 1 • Book 2

Name _____

▶ **Write a letter to a friend. Tell about
yourself and your family. Write special
names and titles correctly.**

_____

**Dear** _____ ,

_____

_____

_____

_____

_____

_____

_____

_____

_____

_____

_____

**Your pal,**

_____

_____

▶ **Circle the special names of places.**
**Write each special name correctly.**

**I.** Jess and Seth go to smith school.

_____

- - - - - - - - - - - - - - - - - - - - - - - - - - - - -

_____


**2.** The best fishing is at apple pond.

_____

- - - - - - - - - - - - - - - - - - - - - - - - - - - - -

_____


**3.** Jed will run to rock hill.

_____

- - - - - - - - - - - - - - - - - - - - - - - - - - - - -

_____


**4.** Ellen and Jan met at hilltop shop.

_____

- - - - - - - - - - - - - - - - - - - - - - - - - - - - -

_____


**5.** Matt lives on thorn way.

_____

- - - - - - - - - - - - - - - - - - - - - - - - - - - - -

_____

**Grammar Practice Book**
© Harcourt • Grade 1 • Book 2

▶ **Circle each special name of a place.
Draw a line to match the name to a picture.**

**1.** Sunset Forest
forest

**2.** West School
school

**3.** pond
Windmill Pond

▶ **Complete each sentence with the special name of
a place.**

**4.** I go to school at _____.

_____

**5.** I live on _____.

_____

**6.** I play ball at _____.

**Grammar Practice Book**
© Harcourt • Grade 1 • Book 2

Name _____

▶ **Read about Jill's day. Circle the special names of places. Write each special name correctly.**

**1.** Jill lives on long path.

_____

**2.** She ran up gold hill.

_____

**3.** She swam in hunt pond.

_____

**4.** She rode past grand cliff.

_____

**5.** She met Mom at clam grill.

_____

**Grammar Practice Book**
© Harcourt • Grade 1 • Book 2

▶ **Circle each sentence that is written
correctly.**

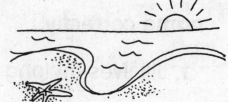

1. Hank lives on York Way.

2. Beth lives by flag cliff.

3. Trish lives next to the Red Mitten Store.

4. Todd lives by sunset shore.

5. Dennis and Jen live on top of Rust Hill.

▶ **Now write the other sentences correctly.**

6. _____

_____

_____

7. _____

_____

_____

Name _____

**Names of Days and Months**
**Lesson 13**

▶ **Read each sentence. Circle the name of the month. Then write the name of the month correctly.**

1. We get wet in april.

2. We camp in june.

3. It is hot in july.

4. We go to school in september.

5. We have hot drinks in december.

**Grammar Practice Book**
© Harcourt • Grade 1 • Book 3

► **Read each sentence. Circle the name of the day. Then write the name of the day correctly.**

**1.** I will go to school on monday.

_____

- - - - - - - - - - - - - - - - - -

_____

**2.** On tuesday, we will see animals.

_____

- - - - - - - - - - - - - - - - - -

_____

**3.** A vet will visit on wednesday.

_____

- - - - - - - - - - - - - - - - - -

_____

**4.** Our class will get a pet on thursday.

_____

- - - - - - - - - - - - - - - - - -

_____

**5.** We have a math test on friday.

_____

- - - - - - - - - - - - - - - - - -

_____

**Grammar Practice Book**
© Harcourt • Grade 1 • Book 3

Name _____

► **Look at the picture. Then complete each sentence correctly.**

MONDAY
TUESDAY
WEDNESDAY
THURSDAY
FRIDAY
SATURDAY
SUNDAY

This is Wednesday.
Let's water the plants.

_____
- - - - - - - - - - - - - - - - -

1. This is _____.

_____
_____
- - - - - - - - - - - - - - - - -

2. The next day is _____.

_____
_____
- - - - - - - - - - - - - - - - -

3. Then it will be _____.

_____
_____
- - - - - - - - - - - - - - - - -

4. The day I like best is _____.

▶ **Write sentences about your favorite
two months. Tell what you like to do during
each month. Write the sentences correctly.**

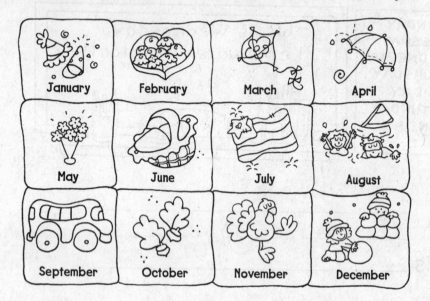

January   February   March   April

May   June   July   August

September   October   November   December

_____

1. _____

_____

_____

_____

2. _____

_____

_____

▶ **Circle the correct way to write the name of each holiday. Then write it.**

**1.** new year's day
New Year's Day

_____

- - - - - - - - - - - - - - - - - -

_____

_____

**2.** Memorial Day
memorial day

_____

- - - - - - - - - - - - - - - - - -

_____

_____

**3.** independence day
Independence Day

_____

- - - - - - - - - - - - - - - - - -

_____

_____

**4.** Thanksgiving Day
thanksgiving day

_____

- - - - - - - - - - - - - - - - - -

_____

_____

▶ **Write the holiday name in each sentence correctly.**

**1.** We'll sing a song on flag day.

_____

- - - - - - - - - - - - - - - - - - - - - - - - - - - - -

_____

_____

**2.** We have a picnic on memorial day.

_____

- - - - - - - - - - - - - - - - - - - - - - - - - - - - -

_____

_____

**3.** Gram visits us on thanksgiving day.

_____

- - - - - - - - - - - - - - - - - - - - - - - - - - - - -

_____

_____

**4.** We'll act in a play on columbus day.

_____

- - - - - - - - - - - - - - - - - - - - - - - - - - - - -

_____

_____

▶ **Circle each sentence that is written correctly.**

1. We eat at home on Thanksgiving Day.

2. This flag is for flag day.

3. I plant a tree on arbor day.

4. Robin made lunch for Dad on Father's Day.

5. It was hot on Independence Day.

▶ **Now write the other sentences correctly.**

6. _____

7. _____

Name _____

▶ **Write three sentences about your favorite holidays. Write the names of the holidays correctly.**

1. _____
_ _ _ _ _ _ _ _ _ _ _ _ _ _ _ _ _ _ _ _ _ _
_____
_ _ _ _ _ _ _ _ _ _ _ _ _ _ _ _ _ _ _ _ _ _
_____

2. _____
_____
_ _ _ _ _ _ _ _ _ _ _ _ _ _ _ _ _ _ _ _ _ _
_____
_____
_ _ _ _ _ _ _ _ _ _ _ _ _ _ _ _ _ _ _ _ _ _

3. _____
_____
_ _ _ _ _ _ _ _ _ _ _ _ _ _ _ _ _ _ _ _ _ _
_____

▶ **Circle the naming part of each sentence. Underline the telling part of each sentence. Then write the sentence correctly.**

**1.** tom bumped me

_____

- - - - - - - - - - - - - - - - - - - - - -

_____

**2.** i fell on the grass

_____

- - - - - - - - - - - - - - - - - - - - - -

_____

**3.** he helped me up

_____

- - - - - - - - - - - - - - - - - - - - - -

_____

**4.** i like tom

_____

- - - - - - - - - - - - - - - - - - - - - -

_____

▶ **Circle the correct word that completes each sentence. Then write the word.**

I        me
_____

1. Rick and _____ do chores.
_____

I        me
_____

2. _____ get some rags.
_____

I        me
_____

3. Rick helps _____ dust.
_____

I        me
_____

4. He and _____ like to dust.
_____

I        me
_____

5. Mom thanks Rick and _____.

**Grammar Practice Book**
© Harcourt • Grade 1 • Book 3

Name _____

► **Circle each word group that belongs in the naming part of a sentence.**

1. Cal and I

2. Ellen and me

3. Mom and me

4. you and I

5. you and me

► **Choose three of the word groups and add words to them to make sentences. Write the sentences correctly.**

6. _____

_____

7. _____

_____

8. _____

**Grammar Practice Book**
© Harcourt • Grade 1 • Book 3

▶ **Complete the sentence, using I or me.**
**Write the sentence correctly.**

I. _____ like to swim

_____

- - - - - - - - - - - - - - - - - - - -

_____

2. my chicks swim with _____

_____

- - - - - - - - - - - - - - - - - - - -

_____

- - - - - - - - - - - - - - - - - - - -

_____

3. _____ can quack

_____

- - - - - - - - - - - - - - - - - - - -

_____

4. you can see _____

_____

- - - - - - - - - - - - - - - - - - - -

_____

5. _____ am a duck.

_____

- - - - - - - - - - - - - - - - - - - -

_____

**Grammar Practice Book**
© Harcourt • Grade 1 • Book 3

Name _____

▶ **Read each sentence. Write the pronoun that matches the underlined words.**

1. <u>Frank</u> fixes eggs. _____

   _____

2. <u>Helen</u> runs by the park. _____

   _____

3. <u>Brent and Ed</u> print cards. _____

   _____

4. <u>The farm</u> has pigs. _____

   _____

5. <u>The bell</u> rings softly. _____

   _____

6. <u>The children</u> are happy. _____

61

► **Label the picture with the correct pronoun.**

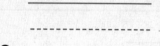

1. _____

2. _____

3. _____

4. _____

► **Use a pronoun to write a sentence about one of the pictures.**

5. _____

**Grammar Practice Book**
© Harcourt • Grade 1 • Book 3

▶ **Read each sentence. Underline the noun or nouns. Use the correct pronoun to complete the next sentence.**

_____

1. Dan is at the park. _____ has his mitt.

_____

_____

2. Gwen brings her softball. _____ sees Dan.

_____

_____

3. Dan and Gwen run to the grass. _____ will play catch.

_____

_____

4. The park is big. _____ has lots of grass.

_____

_____

5. Gwen sees a star. _____ knows it will be dark soon.

_____

_____

6. Dan picks up the ball and mitt. _____ will take them to his house.

**Grammar Practice Book**
© Harcourt • Grade 1 • Book 3

▶ **Circle each sentence pair that is written correctly.**

1. Karl is at the pond. He sits on a bench.

2. Mark and Tom play. He are friends.

3. Beth fixes popcorn. He drinks milk, too.

4. There is a nest. It is on a branch.

▶ **Now write the other sentences. Write the pronouns correctly.**

5. _____
   _____
   _____
   _____

6. _____
   _____
   _____
   _____

▶ **Complete the sentences. Write the possessive noun correctly.**

**squirrel**

_____

1. Did you see the _____ nest?

_____

**Brent**

_____

2. We are in _____ pumpkin patch.

_____

**Sam**

_____

3. Where is _____ shirt?

_____

**dog**

_____

4. The _____ fur is soft.

_____

**Kirk**

_____

5. Is that _____ backpack?

65

▶ **Circle the possessive <u>noun</u> in the first sentence. Then write the possessive <u>pronoun</u> that completes the second sentence.**

**1.** That is Lester's pen.

_____

_____

It is _____ pen.

_____

**2.** Where is Meg's lunch?

_____

_____

Is that _____ lunch?

_____

**3.** I see Pam's marble.

_____

_____

_____ marble is on the desk.

_____

**4.** That is Robert's food.

_____

_____

Robert will eat _____ food.

► **Choose a possessive pronoun from the box to complete each sentence.**

| his | her | your | yours | its | their |
|-----|-----|------|-------|-----|-------|

**I.** I see a bird's nest. _____ nest is in a tree.

**2.** The boys have a tent. That is _____ tent.

**3.** This is my scarf. _____ scarf is over there.

**4.** Jill has a duck. _____ duck quacks a lot.

**5.** Rob juggles blocks. The blocks are _____ .

**6.** This is my lunch. Where is _____?

**Grammar Practice Book**
© Harcourt • Grade 1 • Book 3

▶ **Circle each sentence that is written correctly.**

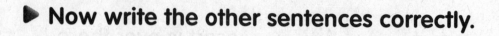

**I.** Tom buckles its belt

**2.** Ella pets her turtle.

**3.** Ben and Mom pack their bags.

**4.** The bobcat licks yours fur.

**5.** Is this magnet yours?

▶ **Now write the other sentences correctly.**

**6.** _____

_____

_____

**7.** _____

_____

▶ **Write the word from the box that completes each sentence.**

| ant | too | new | one | sun | our |
|-----|-----|-----|-----|-----|-----|

**1.** I just got a doll. It is _____.

_____

**2.** The _____ is very small.

_____

**3.** It is hot. The _____ is out.

_____

**4.** We like Jan. She is _____ friend.

_____

**5.** I only have _____ pen.

_____

**6.** This string is _____ long.

▶ **Complete each sentence with the correct homophone from the box.**

1. I can _____ the stars now.

   I can swim in the _____.

   | sea | see |

2. Morris _____ a book.

   Ellen has a _____ jacket.

   | read | red |

3. What is the _____ of one and ten?

   Grab _____ apples from the bucket.

   | some | sum |

4. We will stop at that _____.

   My lunch is _____ a bag.

   | in | inn |

▶ **Read the chart. Choose the correct
homophone from the chart to
complete each sentence.**

| fir | fur |
|------|--------|
| there | their |
| cent | sent |
| mist | missed |

_____
-------------------------------

**1.** The cat has soft _____.

_____
-------------------------------

**2.** Dad went to work. I _____ him.

_____
-------------------------------

**3.** I will sit here. You can sit _____.

_____
-------------------------------

**4.** Mom _____ me to school.

**Grammar Practice Book**
© Harcourt • Grade 1 • Book 3

▶ **Choose a pair of homophones from the chart. Write sentences using the words correctly.**

| | |
|---|---|
| buy | by |
| to | two |
| wax | whacks |

1. _____

_____

_____

2. _____

_____

_____

Name _____

▶ **Read the ad. Find color words and size words. Write them in the chart.**

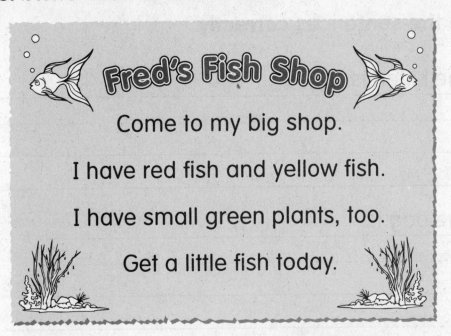

Fred's Fish Shop

Come to my big shop.

I have red fish and yellow fish.

I have small green plants, too.

Get a little fish today.

| Color Words | Size Words |
|---|---|
| _____ | _____ |
| _____ | _____ |
| _____ | _____ |
| _____ | _____ |
| _____ | _____ |
| _____ | _____ |

Name _____

▶ **Add words describing color, size or shape to complete each sentence. Write the sentences correctly.**

**1.** the kitten is

_____

- - - - - - - - - - - - - - - - - - - - - - - - - - - - - - - - - -

_____

_____

**2.** the dog is

_____

- - - - - - - - - - - - - - - - - - - - - - - - - - - - - - - - - -

_____

_____

**3.** the bus is

_____

- - - - - - - - - - - - - - - - - - - - - - - - - - - - - - - - - -

_____

_____

**4.** the ball is

_____

- - - - - - - - - - - - - - - - - - - - - - - - - - - - - - - - - -

_____

_____

**5.** the socks are

_____

- - - - - - - - - - - - - - - - - - - - - - - - - - - - - - - - - -

_____

**Grammar Practice Book**
© Harcourt • Grade 1 • Book 4

▶ **Circle each sentence that has a describing word.**

**1.** I see a long van.

**2.** The truck is red.

**3.** The bus went past.

**4.** Here is a cab.

**5.** A tire is flat.

▶ **Add describing words to the other sentences. Write the sentences correctly.**

**6.** _____
_____
_____

**7.** _____
_____
_____

**Grammar Practice Book**
© Harcourt • Grade 1 • Book 4

Name _____

▶ **Write two sentences that tell about
things in the picture. Use describing
words in each sentence.**

1. _____
_____
_____

2. _____
_____
_____

**Grammar Practice Book**
© Harcourt • Grade 1 • Book 4

Name _____

▶ **Read the chart of describing words. Write the word from the chart that best completes each sentence.**

| | | | |
|---|---|---|---|
| sweet | fresh | soft | hard |
| hot | bad | loud | wet |

1. _____ taste _____ .

2. The _____ smells _____ .

3. The _____ feel _____ .

4. The _____ makes a _____ sound.

5. The _____ smells _____ .

77

Grammar Practice Book

▶ **Complete each sentence, using a describing word. Write the sentences.**

1. the water feels _____
   _____
   - - - - - - - - - - - - - - - - - - - - - - - - - - - -
   _____

2. the jam tastes _____
   _____
   - - - - - - - - - - - - - - - - - - - - - - - - - - - -
   _____

3. the corn smells _____
   _____
   - - - - - - - - - - - - - - - - - - - - - - - - - - - -
   _____

▶ **Write a sentence about how something sounds. Use a describing word.**

   _____
   - - - - - - - - - - - - - - - - - - - - - - - - - - - -
4. _____
   _____
   - - - - - - - - - - - - - - - - - - - - - - - - - - - -
   _____

▶ **Read each group of words. Draw a
line under each describing word.**

1. sweet muffin

2. pretty wings

3. clanging bells

4. thundering yell

5. dry dirt

▶ **Use two of the word groups above to make
sentences. Write the sentences correctly.**

6. _____

_____

_____

7. _____

_____

_____

79

Grammar Practice Book
© Harcourt • Grade 1 • Book 4

Name _____

▶ **Use describing words to write a sentence about each picture. Write the sentences correctly.**

1.

   _____
   - - - - - - - - - - - - - - - -
   _____
   - - - - - - - - - - - - - - - -
   _____

   _____

2.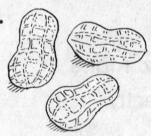

   _____
   - - - - - - - - - - - - - - - -
   _____
   - - - - - - - - - - - - - - - -
   _____

   _____

3.

   _____
   - - - - - - - - - - - - - - - -
   _____
   - - - - - - - - - - - - - - - -
   _____

**Grammar Practice Book**
© Harcourt • Grade 1 • Book 4

▶ **Read the sentences. Circle the word that tells how many. Then circle how many Chester will eat.**

**1.** Chester will eat two peanuts.

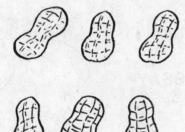

**2.** Chester will have one apple.

**3.** Chester will gobble four raisins.

**4.** Chester will take three muffins.

Grammar Practice Book
© Harcourt • Grade 1 • Book 4

▶ **Look at the pictures. Then complete each sentence. Write the word that tells how many.**

_____

1. Mark saw _____ birds.

_____

2. I will eat _____ grapes.

_____

3. Pat has _____ cats.

_____

4. I see _____ rainbow.

_____

5. Jen has _____ stamps.

▶ **Look at the picture. Complete each sentence with the correct number of animals.**

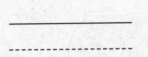

_____
------------------

1. There are _____ ducks.

_____
------------------

2. There is _____ eagle.

_____
------------------

3. There are _____ turtles.

_____
------------------

4. There are _____ frogs.

▶ **Write a sentence about another kind of animal. Use a word that tells how many.**

5. _____
---------------------------------
_____
---------------------------------
_____

**Grammar Practice Book**
© Harcourt • Grade 1 • Book 4

▶ **Look at the picture. Write sentences that tell what you see. Use words that tell how many.**

1. _____

2. _____

3. _____

4. _____

5. _____

Name ______________________________



▶ **Circle each word that describes a feeling. Write each sentence correctly.**

**1.** dad was surprised

**2.** mom was hungry

**3.** i felt sad

**4.** jack was happy


© Harcourt • Grade 1 • Book 4

▶ **Choose the word that best completes the sentence. Write the word.**

sad     hungry

_____
- - - - - - - - - - - - - - - - - - - - - - - - - - -

**1.** My cat is lost. I feel _____.

_____

mean     happy

_____
- - - - - - - - - - - - - - - - - - - - - - - - - - -

**2.** It is my birthday. I feel _____.

_____

good     bad

_____
- - - - - - - - - - - - - - - - - - - - - - - - - - -

**3.** I am sick. I feel _____.

_____

▶ **Use another feeling word in a sentence.**

_____
- - - - - - - - - - - - - - - - - - - - - - - - - - - - - - - -

**4.** _____

_____
- - - - - - - - - - - - - - - - - - - - - - - - - - - - - - - -

_____

▶ **Circle the feeling word in each sentence.**

**1.** My class is glad.

**2.** I am sad.

**3.** The teacher is happy.

**4.** Greg is tired.

▶ **Use feeling words to complete each sentence below.**

**5.** I smile when I am _____.

_____

**6.** I eat when I am _____.

_____

**7.** I rest when I am _____.

**Grammar Practice Book**
© Harcourt • Grade 1 • Book 4

▶ **Complete the sentences with feeling words.**

_____
-------------------------------

1. When I play, I feel _____.

_____
-------------------------------

2. When I get a gift, I am _____.

_____
-------------------------------

3. When I sing a song, I feel _____.

▶ **Write sentences to describe each picture. Use feeling words.**

4. _____
   -------------------------------
   _____
   -------------------------------

5. _____
   -------------------------------
   _____
   -------------------------------

**Grammar Practice Book**
© Harcourt • Grade 1 • Book 4

Name _____

▶ **Add <u>er</u> or <u>est</u> to the word to complete the sentence. Write the word.**

tall
_____
- - - - - - - - - - - - - - - - - - - - - - - -

**1.** That bird sits in the _____ tree in the forest.

_____

big
_____
- - - - - - - - - - - - - - - - - - - - - - -

**2.** My desk is the _____ in the room.

_____

dark
_____
- - - - - - - - - - - - - - - - - - - - - - -

**3.** My dog has _____ fur than my cat.

_____

small
_____
- - - - - - - - - - - - - - - - - - - - - - -

**4.** A cat is _____ than a goat.

_____

short
_____
- - - - - - - - - - - - - - - - - - - - - - -

**5.** I am _____ than my sister.

**Grammar Practice Book**
© Harcourt • Grade 1 • Book 4

► **Look at the pictures. Add <u>er</u> or <u>est</u> to a word from the box to complete each sentence.**

| fast     slow |
|---|

_____
- - - - - - - - - - - - - - - - - - - - - - - - - -

**1.** The raft is _____ than the speedboat.

_____
- - - - - - - - - - - - - - - - - - - - - - - - - -

**2.** The sailboat is _____ than the raft.

_____
- - - - - - - - - - - - - - - - - - - - - - - - - -

**3.** The speedboat is _____ of all.

_____
- - - - - - - - - - - - - - - - - - - - - - - - - -

**4.** The raft is _____ of all.

▶ **Draw pictures of three animals. Show how they compare in size. Label each picture using words from the box.**

| big | bigger | biggest |
|-----|--------|---------|

_____

- - - - - - - - - - - - -

_____

**Grammar Practice Book**
© Harcourt • Grade 1 • Book 4

▶ **Look at the picture. Write sentences that compare the animals. Use words that end in <u>er</u> and <u>est</u>.**

1. _____

_____

_____

2. _____

_____

_____

3. _____

_____

_____

▶ **Read each sentence, and look at each underlined word. Circle the picture that shows the meaning the word has in the sentence. Then write the word on the line.**

_____

**1.** The <u>ring</u> fits my finger. _____

_____

**2.** Dad will <u>park</u> the car. _____

_____

**3.** I like to <u>fish</u>. _____

_____

**4.** The <u>bat</u> flew to the cave. _____

**Grammar Practice Book**
© Harcourt • Grade 1 • Book 4

Name _____

▶ **Choose the word that will complete both sentences. Write that word in each sentence.**

**1. fast   left**

_____

- - - - - - - - - - - - - - - - - - -

Turn _____ at the next street.

_____

- - - - - - - - - - - - - - - -

I _____ my coat at school.

**2. inches   feet**

The yarn is six

_____

- - - - - - - - - - - - - - - -

_____ long.

Bev and Jim stamp their

_____

- - - - - - - - - - - - - - - -

_____ .

**3. pond   store**

Ben and I went to the

_____

- - - - - - - - - - - - - - - -

_____ .

_____

- - - - - - - - - - - - - - - -

Animals _____ food for the winter.

**4. desk   sink**

The glasses are in the

_____

- - - - - - - - - - - - - - - -

_____ .

_____

- - - - - - - - - - - - - - - -

Rocks _____ in water.

94

▶ **Read each sentence. Underline the word that can have two meanings. Circle the picture that shows how the word is used in the sentence.**

**1.** The dog ran around the yard.

**2.** The pig was kept in a pen.

**3.** I had to duck out of the way.

▶ **Write a sentence for <u>can</u>. Make it clear which meaning you used.**

**4.** _____

_____

_____

▶ **Draw pictures to show two meanings of each word. Choose one meaning, and write a sentence that shows it.**

1. bump

_____
- - - - - - - - - - - - - - - - - - - - - - -
_____
_____
- - - - - - - - - - - - - - - - - - - - - - -
_____

2. wave

_____
- - - - - - - - - - - - - - - - - - - - - - -
_____
_____
- - - - - - - - - - - - - - - - - - - - - - -
_____

▶ **Circle the verb in each sentence.**
**Then write the sentences correctly.**

**1.** a rabbit hops _____

-----------------------------------

-----------------------------------

**2.** my fish blows bubbles _____

-----------------------------------

-----------------------------------

-----------------------------------

**3.** the cat dozes _____

-----------------------------------

-----------------------------------

**4.** the red bird flutters _____

-----------------------------------

-----------------------------------

-----------------------------------

**5.** the pup wiggles _____

-----------------------------------

-----------------------------------

▶ **Write an interesting verb to complete each sentence.**

_____
- - - - - - - - - - - - - - - - - - - - - - - - - - - - -

1. I _____ to the park.

_____
- - - - - - - - - - - - - - - - - - - - - - - - - - - - -

2. We _____ our lunch.

_____
- - - - - - - - - - - - - - - - - - - - - - - - - - - - -

3. Nate will _____ home.

_____
- - - - - - - - - - - - - - - - - - - - - - - - - - - - -

4. We _____ across the room.

_____
- - - - - - - - - - - - - - - - - - - - - - - - - - - - -

5. They _____ around the yard.

▶ **Circle each group of words that is a complete sentence.**

   **I.** We hiked to the animal park.

   **2.** The goats their food.

   **3.** We to the snake house.

   **4.** The bats were asleep.

   **5.** June and I baked a cake.

▶ **Add verbs to the other groups of words to make sentences. Write the sentences correctly.**

   **6.** _____

_____

_____

   **7.** _____

_____

_____

**Grammar Practice Book**
© Harcourt • Grade 1 • Book 5

Name ____________________



▶ **Use verbs from the box. Write sentences that tell what animals do.**

| | | | |
|---|---|---|---|
| leap | jump | wiggle | lick |
| bite | paddle | swim | dive |
| slither | sleep | cuddle | gobble |
| flop | | | |

**1.** ____________________

**2.** ____________________

**3.** ____________________

▶ **Write the verb that completes
each sentence.**

**swim    swims**

_____

- - - - - - - - - - - - - - - - - -

**I.** One octopus _____ in the water.

_____

**play    plays**

_____

- - - - - - - - - - - - - - - - - -

**2.** The seals _____ with a ball.

_____

**swing    swings**

_____

- - - - - - - - - - - - - - - - - -

**3.** Elephants _____ their trunks.

_____

**slap    slaps**

_____

- - - - - - - - - - - - - - - - - -

**4.** The beaver _____ his tail.

_____

**run    runs**

_____

- - - - - - - - - - - - - - - - - -

**5.** We _____ to see the next animal.

Name _____

▶ **Circle the sentences that use the verb correctly.**

**1.** We play soccer at school.

**2.** Tess run fast to get the ball.

**3.** I kick the ball to my friend.

**4.** Bob score a goal.

**5.** We win the game this time.

▶ **Now correct the verbs in the other sentences. Write the sentences correctly.**

_____

**6.** _____

_____

_____

_____

**7.** _____

102

Name _____

▶ **Read the story. Then complete each sentence with the correct verb from the box.**

| crawls | jumps | races | see |
|--------|-------|-------|-----|
| sings | sit | throws | |

### At the Park

I _____ a black beetle. It _____

_____ on a leaf. A bird _____ a song. Three

_____ little birds _____ in a nest. A dog

_____ past me. A boy _____ a

_____ stick. The dog _____ up to catch it.

103

Name _____

▶ **Use verbs from the chart to write
sentences that tell about now.**

| plant | grow | fall | dig | pick |
| plants | grows | falls | digs | picks |

1. _____

_____

_____

_____

2. _____

_____

_____

_____

3. _____

_____

_____

Name _____

▶ **Read each sentence. Circle <u>one</u> or more than one to show how many people or things the sentence is about. Then write <u>am</u>, <u>is</u>, or <u>are</u> to complete the sentence.**

_____
- - - - - - - - - - - -

**1.** I _____ Rick.

        **one**    **more than one**

_____

_____
- - - - - - - - - - - -

**2.** My best friend _____ Carl.

        **one**    **more than one**

_____

_____
- - - - - - - - - - - -

**3.** We _____ on a team.

        **one**    **more than one**

_____

_____
- - - - - - - - - - - -

**4.** Carl _____ a good batter.

        **one**    **more than one**

_____

_____
- - - - - - - - - - - -

**5.** We _____ happy to be on the team.

        **one**    **more than one**

**Grammar Practice Book**
© Harcourt • Grade 1 • Book 5

▶ **Circle each sentence that is written correctly.**

1. Mom and I are in the garden.

2. Mom is watching a butterfly.

3. Jill and Tom are planting roses.

4. They is watering plants, too.

5. Kevin am picking flowers.

▶ **Write the other sentences correctly.**

_____
-----------------------------------

6. _____

_____
-----------------------------------

_____

_____

_____
-----------------------------------

7. _____

_____
-----------------------------------

_____

► **Draw a line to complete each sentence.**
**Write the completed sentences correctly.**

1. I                                           are in the river.

2. Jane                                     are not with us.

3. Fish                                      am on the bridge.

4. You                                      is in the river.

5. _____

6. _____

7. _____

8. _____

**Grammar Practice Book**
© Harcourt • Grade 1 • Book 5

► **Write am, is, or are to complete each sentence.**

**1.** I _____ riding my bike.

_____

**2.** Mom _____ riding her bike.

_____

**3.** We _____ riding to the pond.

_____

**4.** You _____ going too fast!

_____

**5.** She _____ waiting for me.

Name _____

▶ **Read each sentence. Write the verb
that tells about the past.**

1. Yesterday, we skipped to the park.

_____

- - - - - - - - - - - - - -

_____

_____

2. Dad cooked corn in the pit. _____

- - - - - - - - - - - - - - - - -

_____

_____

- - - - - - - - - - - - - - - - -

3. We played softball on the field. _____

_____

4. When it was dark, we walked home.

_____

- - - - - - - - - - - - - - -

_____

_____

5. We watched the stars come out.

_____

- - - - - - - - - - - - - - - - -

_____

109

▶ **Circle each sentence uses a verb that
tells about the past.**

    **1.** A frog jumped on a log.

    **2.** I look at the frog.

    **3.** I walk past it.

    **4.** The frog croaks.

    **5.** I laughed at the frog.

▶ **Now change the verb in the other sentences
to a verb that tells about the past.
Write the sentences correctly.**

**6.** _____

_____

**7.** _____

_____

**8.** _____

Name _____

▶ **Change each verb in the box to a verb
that tells about the past. Then complete
each sentence with the correct verb.**

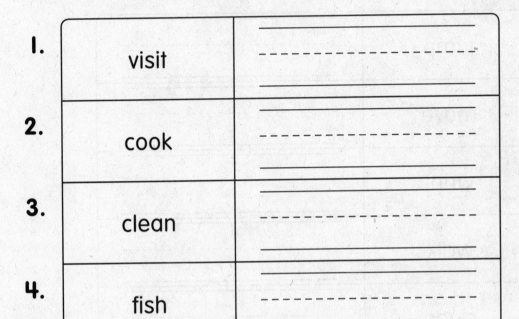

| | | |
|---|---|---|
| **1.** | visit | _____ |
| **2.** | cook | _____ |
| **3.** | clean | _____ |
| **4.** | fish | _____ |

**5.** Last week, I _____ my Granddad.

**6.** We _____ from the bridge.

**7.** We _____ our dinner on a grill.

**8.** I _____ my plate.

111

► **Change each verb in the box to a verb that tells about the past. Then choose one verb and write a sentence about the past.**

| | | |
|---|---|---|
| 1. | jump | ------------------------------ |
| 2. | move | ------------------------------ |
| 3. | want | ------------------------------ |
| 4. | walk | ------------------------------ |
| 5. | clean | ------------------------------ |
| 6. | pick | ------------------------------ |

7. _____

------------------------------

------------------------------

Name _____

▶ **Choose the correct word to go with the verb in each sentence.**

**beaver      beavers**

_____

- - - - - - - - - - - - - - - - - - - - - - - - -

**1.** A _____ was in the creek.

_____

**cat      cats**

_____

- - - - - - - - - - - - - - - - - - - - - - - - -

**2.** Two _____ were chasing a butterfly.

_____

**cow      cows**

_____

- - - - - - - - - - - - - - - - - - - - - - - - -

**3.** The _____ was by the haystack.

_____

**flower      flowers**

_____

- - - - - - - - - - - - - - - - - - - - - - - - -

**4.** Some _____ were in the garden.

_____

**peacock      peacocks**

- - - - - - - - - - - - - - - - - - - - - - - - -

**5.** A _____ was on the path.

**Grammar Practice Book**
© Harcourt • Grade 1 • Book 5

▶ **Circle <u>one</u> or <u>more than one</u> to show how many the sentence is about. Then write <u>was</u> or <u>were</u> to complete each sentence.**

1. Jack and Nate _____ sitting on a bench.

   **one        more than one**

2. Jack _____ quiet.

   **one        more than one**

3. Nate _____ yelling loudly.

   **one        more than one**

4. Jack and Nate _____ fishing.

   **one        more than one**

5. They _____ thinking about fish for dinner.

   **one        more than one**

**Grammar Practice Book**
© Harcourt • Grade 1 • Book 5

▶ **Circle each sentence that uses <u>was</u> or <u>were</u> correctly.**

1. Pete and I was playing in the rain.

2. We were wearing raincoats.

3. My boots and socks was wet.

4. Pete was stamping in the puddles.

5. He was splashing me!

▶ **Write the other sentences correctly.**

6. _____

_____

_____

7. _____

_____

_____

▶ **Write <u>was</u> or <u>were</u> on the lines to complete the story.**

The house _____ messy. It _____ Mom's

birthday. She _____ still at work. Dad and Sandy

_____ cleaning. Arthur _____ making a

big cake. We _____ excited. Soon the house and

the cake _____ ready.

▶ **Use <u>was</u> or <u>were</u> to write a sentence about what happened when Mom came home.**

_____

_____

_____

**Grammar Practice Book**
© Harcourt • Grade 1 • Book 5

▶ **Circle the sentences that are written correctly.**

1. The tiger went into the jungle.

2. Yesterday, we go to the river.

3. Jen go to school last week.

4. You can go with me now.

5. Last night, we went to bed late.

▶ **Now write the other sentences correctly.**

6. _____
_____
_____

7. _____
_____
_____

Name _____

▶ **Write go and went to complete the story.**

**Planning the Party**

_____

Annie _____ to visit Liz last week. They

_____

planned a party. Yesterday, Liz _____ to

the store to buy milk and eggs. Today, Liz and Jan will

_____

_____ to Annie's house. They will make

cupcakes.

▶ **Now, imagine you were invited to the party. Write a sentence to tell what you will do or what you did do. Use go or went correctly.**

_____

_____

_____

_____

_____

**Grammar Practice Book**
© Harcourt • Grade 1 • Book 5

# INDEX

## A

**Adjectives**

*See* Describing words

## C

**Capitalization**

names of days and months, 49–52

names of holidays, 53–56

names of places, 45–48

sentences, 1–4, 17–19, 20–23, 24–26, 27

titles for people, 41–44

**Common nouns**

*See* Nouns, animals or things; people or places

**Complete sentences,** 2–4

## D

**Describing words**

color, size, and shape, 73–76

*-er* and *-est*, 89–92

feelings, 85–88

how many, 81–84

taste, smell, sound, and feel, 77–80

## E

**End marks,** 1–4, 5–8, 17–20, 21–24, 25–28

**Exclamations,** 25–28

## H

**Homophones,** 69–72

## M

**Mechanics**

*See* Capitalization; End marks; Punctuation

## N

**Naming parts of sentences,** 9–12

**Nouns**

animals or things, 33–36

days and months, 49–52

holidays, 53–56

people or places, 29–32

plural nouns, 37–40

possessives, 65–66

proper nouns, 41–44, 45–48, 49–52, 53–56

singular and plural (one and more than one), 37–40

special names and titles for people 41–44

special names of places, 45–48

## P

**Past-tense verbs**

*See* Verbs, that tell about the past

**Plural nouns,** 37–40

**Predicates**

*See* Telling parts of sentences

**Present-tense verbs**

*See* Verbs, that tell about now

**Pronouns**

*he*, *she*, *it*, and *they*, 61–64

*I* and *me*, 57–60

possessive, 67–68

**Punctuation**

    apostrophe in possessive nouns,
      65–66

    end marks, 1–4, 5–8, 17–20, 21–24,
      25–28

## Q

**Questions**, 21–24

## S

**Sentences**

    capital letters and end marks, 1–4,
      5–8, 17–20, 21–24, 25–28

    exclamations, 25–28

    naming parts, 9–12

    questions, 21–24

    telling parts, 13–16

    telling sentences, 17–20

    word order, 5–8

**Subjects**

    *See* Sentences, naming parts

## T

**Telling parts of sentences**, 13–16

**Telling sentences**, 17–20

**Tenses**

    past, 109–112

    present, 101–104

**Titles for people**, 41–44

**Troublesome Words**

    homophones, 69–72

    multiple-meaning words, 93–96

## U

**Usage**

    *am*, *is*, and *are*, 105–108

    *go* and *went*, 117–120

    *was* and *were*, 113–116

## V

**Verbs**, 97–100

    that tell about now, 101–104

    that tell about the past, 109–112

    *am*, *is*, and *are*, 105–108

    *go* and *went*, 117–120

    *was* and *were*, 113–116

## W

**Word Order**, 5–8